PYRAMIDS ALL AROUND THE WORLD

PYRAMIDS KIDS BOOK
CHILDREN'S ANCIENT HISTORY

BABY PROFESSOR
EDUCATION KIDS

Speedy Publishing LLC

40 E. Main St. #1156

Newark, DE 19711

www.speedypublishing.com

Copyright 2017

In this book, we're going to talk about pyramids around the world. So, let's get right to it!

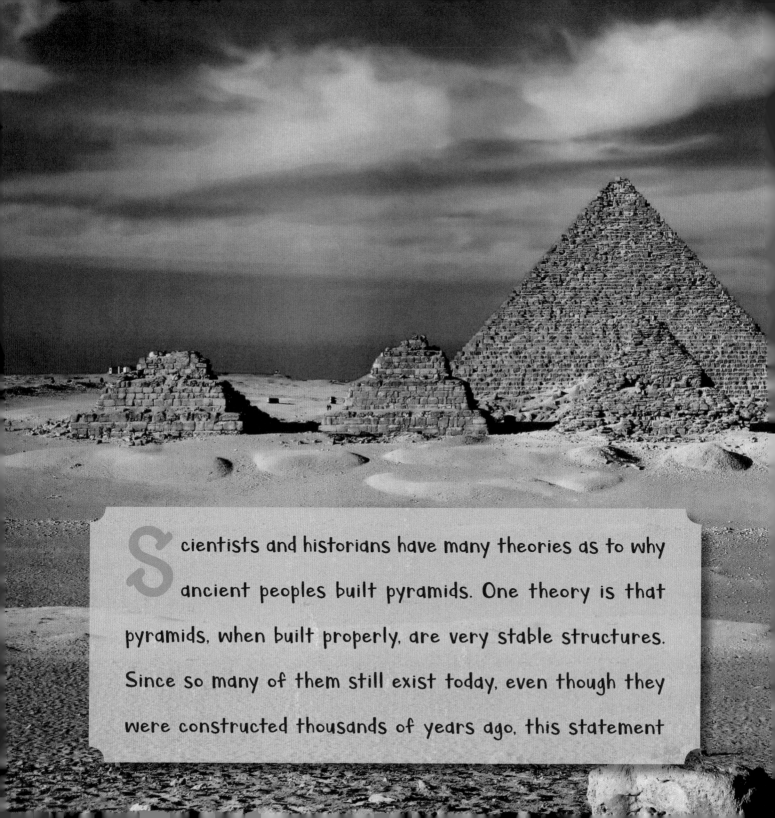

Scientists and historians have many theories as to why ancient peoples built pyramids. One theory is that pyramids, when built properly, are very stable structures. Since so many of them still exist today, even though they were constructed thousands of years ago, this statement

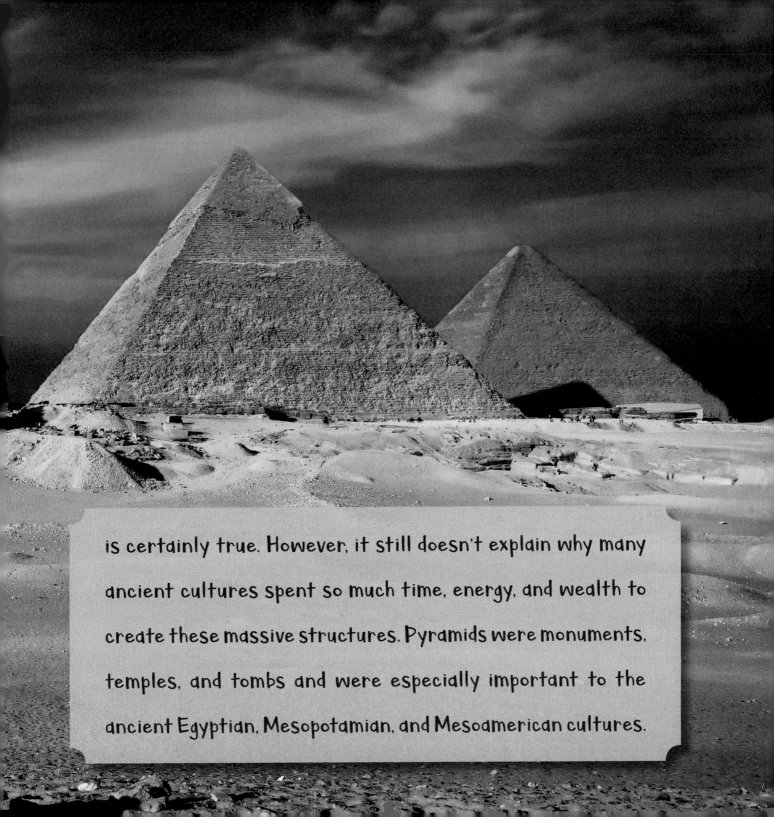

is certainly true. However, it still doesn't explain why many ancient cultures spent so much time, energy, and wealth to create these massive structures. Pyramids were monuments, temples, and tombs and were especially important to the ancient Egyptian, Mesopotamian, and Mesoamerican cultures.

PYRAMID OF DJOSER

The Pyramid of Djoser in Saqqara, Egypt is only one of over 100 different pyramids in that country. It's important to archaeologists and historians because it was the very first pyramid structure constructed in Egypt. It was built when Djoser, the pharaoh who ruled from 2630 to 2611 BC was the leader of Egypt.

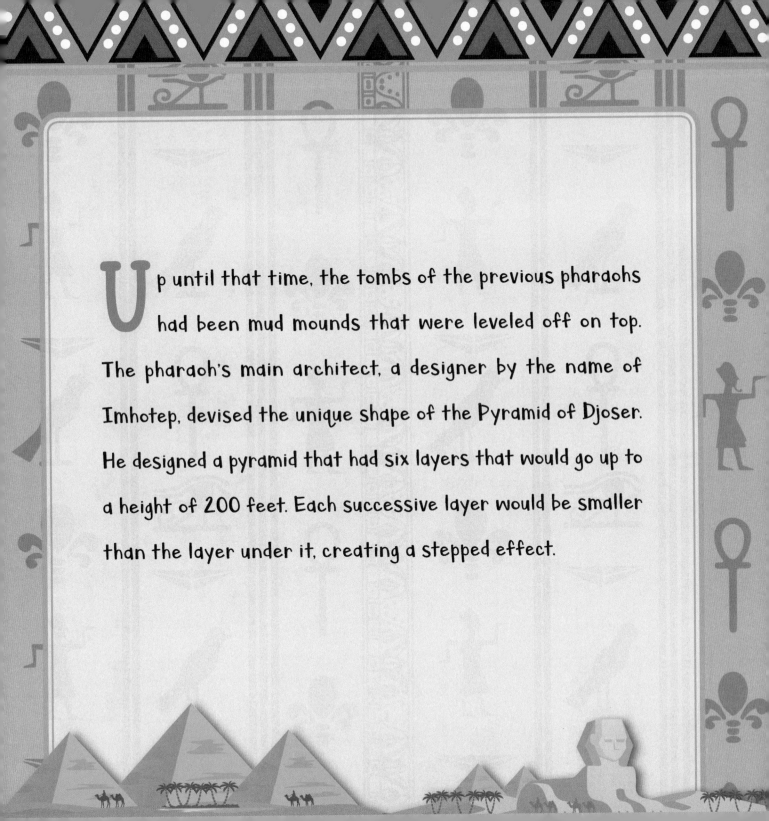

Up until that time, the tombs of the previous pharaohs had been mud mounds that were leveled off on top. The pharaoh's main architect, a designer by the name of Imhotep, devised the unique shape of the Pyramid of Djoser. He designed a pyramid that had six layers that would go up to a height of 200 feet. Each successive layer would be smaller than the layer under it, creating a stepped effect.

Imhotep was a man of many talents. He was also known as a healer and was later worshipped by the Greeks and Romans as a deity of medicine.

PYRAMID OF DJOSER

THE GREAT PYRAMID OF KHUFU

When most people envision pyramids, they think of the three pyramids at Giza in Egypt. This trio of amazing structures rises from the sands of the desert close to the city of modern-day Cairo. Khufu's pyramid, whose ancient name was Khufu's Horizon, is the largest as well as the oldest of the three and is also the northernmost. It was constructed for Khufu who was Egypt's pharaoh around 2551 BC. It is often just called "The Great Pyramid."

It was constructed from over 2 million enormous blocks of stone and its height was once 481 feet, although today it measures at 450 feet in height. For more than 3,000 years it was the tallest structure made by man.

THE GREAT PYRAMID OF KHUFU

PYRAMID'S ENTRANCE DOOR

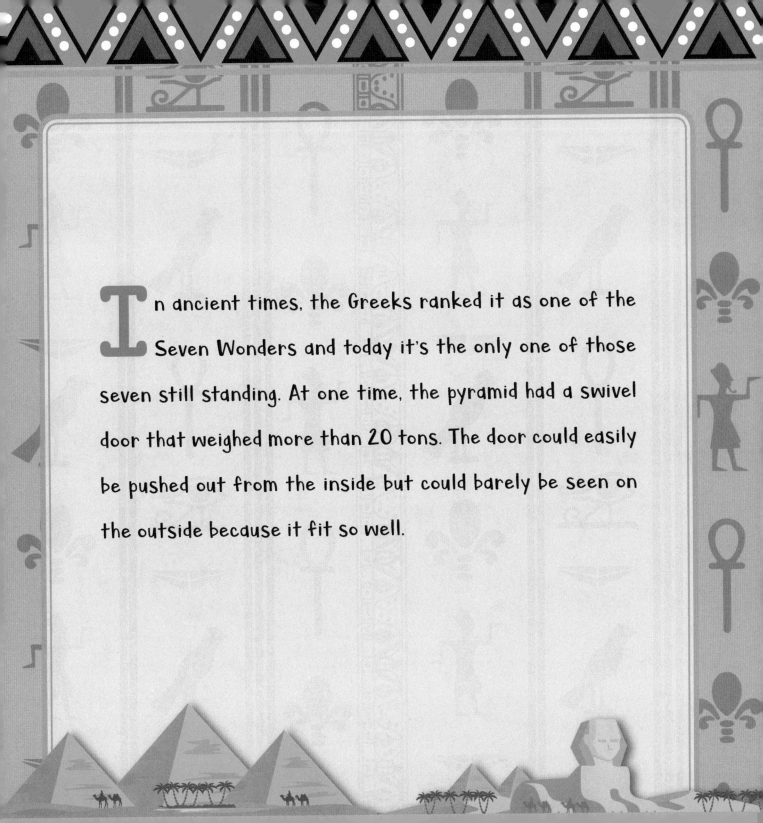

In ancient times, the Greeks ranked it as one of the Seven Wonders and today it's the only one of those seven still standing. At one time, the pyramid had a swivel door that weighed more than 20 tons. The door could easily be pushed out from the inside but could barely be seen on the outside because it fit so well.

THE PYRAMID OF KHAFRE

The Pyramid of Khafre is the middle pyramid of the three Giza pyramids. It was built for Khufu's son around 2520 BC. Although it is not as tall as Khufu's pyramid since it is only 471 feet, it appears to be taller than it is, because the ground it was built on was at a higher elevation.

STATUE OF SPHINX

The temple is surrounded by an elaborate complex of buildings including the mysterious Sphinx. This unusual seated statue has the body of a lion, a human face that once had a nose, and a pharaoh's headdress.

THE CHAVIN TEMPLE COMPLEX

The Chavin Temple Complex is located at the archaeological site of Chavin de Huantar, which is in the Peruvian highlands. It was constructed over several centuries by the Chavin people who lived in the pre-Columbian age circa 900 to 200 BC.

CHAVIN TEMPLE COMPLEX

UNDERGROUND TUNNEL
WITHIN THE TEMPLE

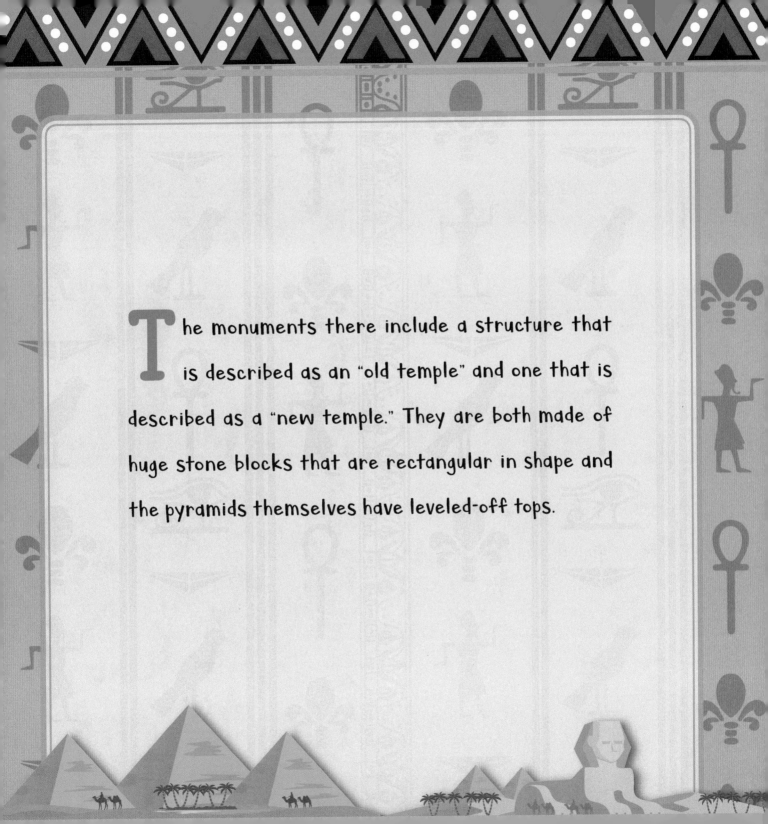

The monuments there include a structure that is described as an "old temple" and one that is described as a "new temple." They are both made of huge stone blocks that are rectangular in shape and the pyramids themselves have leveled-off tops.

The construction at the site includes detailed carvings and passageways as well as channels built for water. Archaeologists believe these structures were used for religious ceremonies.

Even though the site's buildings are today mostly in ruins, historical information shows that Spanish explorers in the 16th century were so amazed by the structures that they thought a race of giants had built them.

UNDERGROUND TUNNEL
WITHIN THE TEMPLE

PYRAMID OF THE SUN

THE PYRAMID OF THE SUN

Around the first century AD, the ancient people of Teotihuacan, Mexico built an amazing pyramid complex. It was built about 1,000 years before the Aztecs settled there and made the city their own. Little is known about its original builders. However, the amazing pyramids they left that are still standing are a testament to their amazing design and building skills.

Their city was planned out and covered more than seven square miles. They built a number of pyramids, but the most monumental is the Pyramid of the Sun, which rises to a height of 200 feet from a square base that is 730 feet

per side. It has five layers of steps. It's located next to the central road of the city called the Avenue of the Dead. The Avenue of the Dead runs south from another massive pyramid in the complex called the Pyramid of the Moon.

THE NUBIAN PYRAMIDS

The leaders of ancient Kush built the Nubian pyramids. They were named after a region in the Nile Valley,

which at one time was called Nubia but today is modern-day Sudan. About 250 narrow pyramids were built with red sandstone at three different sites in Nubia over several hundred years.

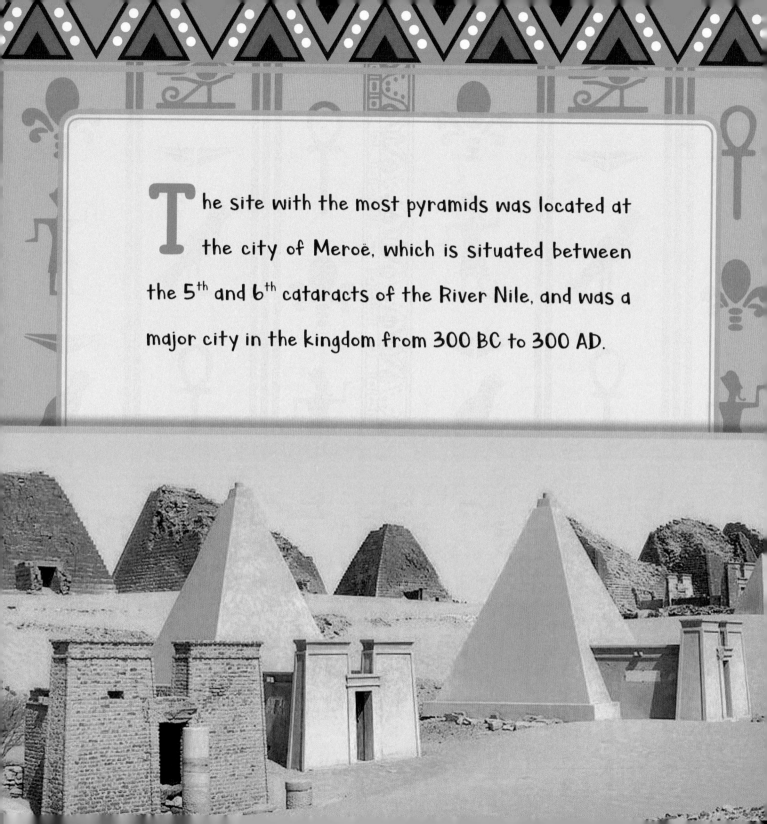

The site with the most pyramids was located at the city of Meroë, which is situated between the 5th and 6th cataracts of the River Nile, and was a major city in the kingdom from 300 BC to 300 AD.

NUBIAN PYRAMIDS

Unfortunately, in the 1830s an Italian doctor and treasure hunter by the name of Giuseppe Ferlini destroyed the tops of 40 of the pyramid tombs in his quest for treasure. Despite this, the ruins are still amazing to see.

NUBIAN PYRAMIDS

THE GREAT PYRAMID OF CHOLULA

The Great Pyramid of Cholula in the state of Puebla in Mexico looks like a grassy mountain. Hidden under the grass and beneath a Catholic Church that was built in the 16th century is one of the largest ancient pyramid complexes in the world.

RUINS OF CHOLULA PYRAMID WITH CHURCH OF OUR LADY OF REMEDIES

It covers a site that is about 45 acres in size and the pyramid itself rises to a height of 177 feet. Its actual name is Tlachihualtepetl, which means "manmade mountain."

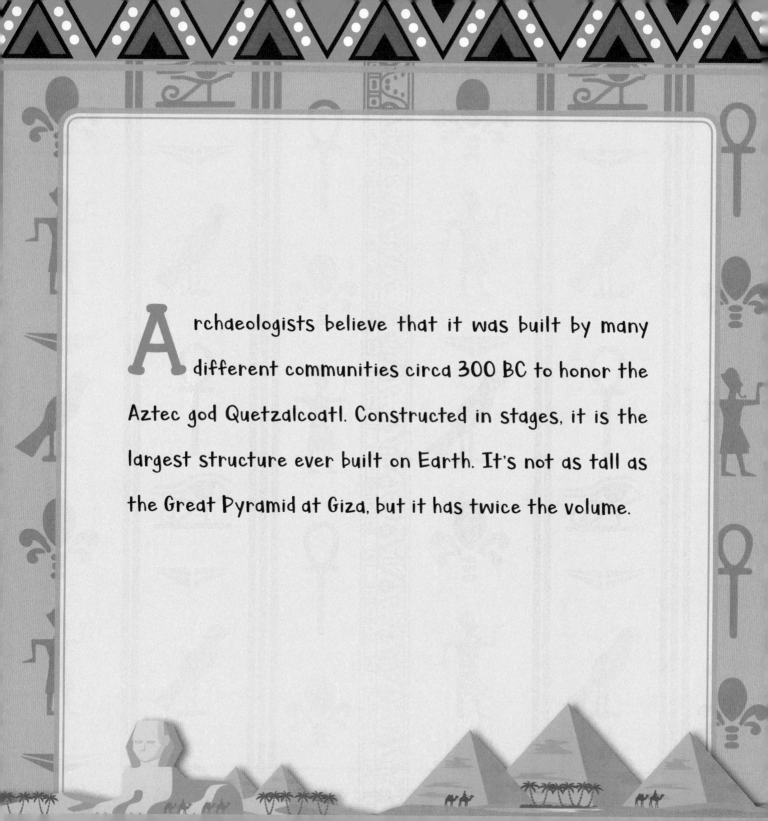

Archaeologists believe that it was built by many different communities circa 300 BC to honor the Aztec god Quetzalcoatl. Constructed in stages, it is the largest structure ever built on Earth. It's not as tall as the Great Pyramid at Giza, but it has twice the volume.

CHURCH OF OUR LADY OF REMEDIES

INSIDE THE GREAT PYRAMID OF CHOLULA

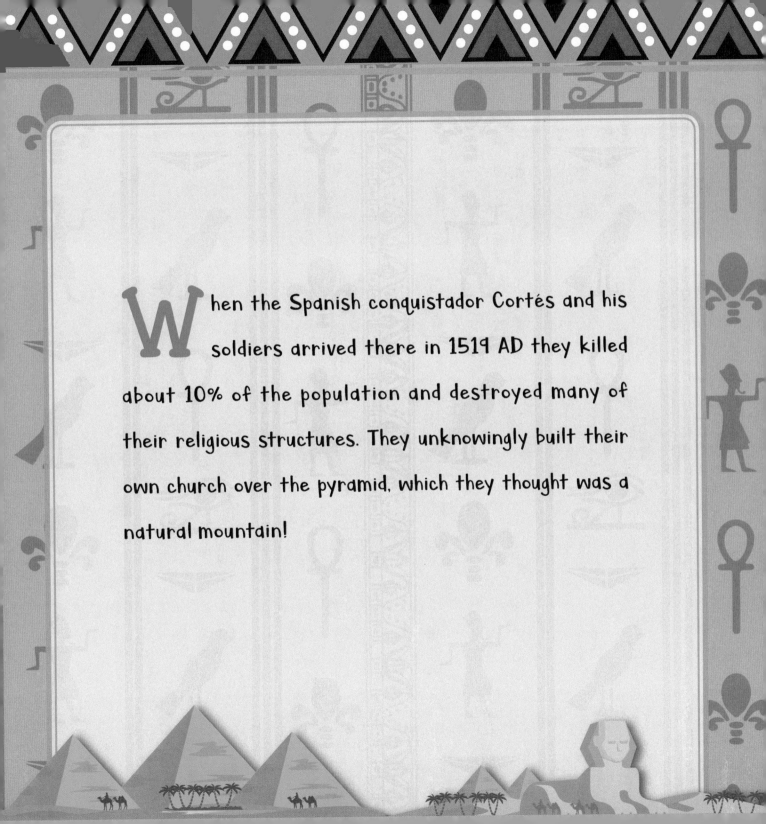

When the Spanish conquistador Cortés and his soldiers arrived there in 1519 AD they killed about 10% of the population and destroyed many of their religious structures. They unknowingly built their own church over the pyramid, which they thought was a natural mountain!

THE ZIGGURAT OF UR

Located in modern-day Iraq, the Ziggurat of Ur was built for Ur-Nammu, one of the kings of Sumeria, around 2100 BC. At one time, it had three stepped-up terraces of

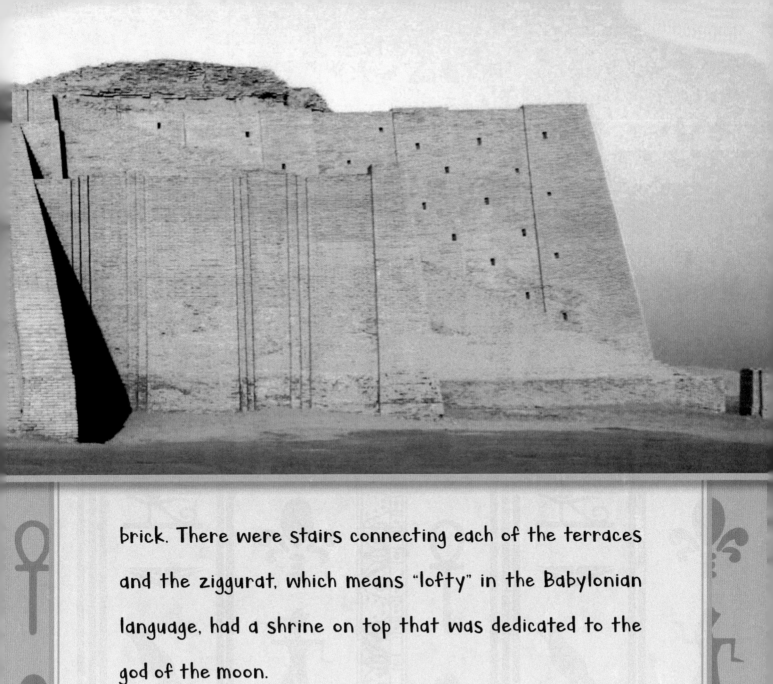

brick. There were stairs connecting each of the terraces and the ziggurat, which means "lofty" in the Babylonian language, had a shrine on top that was dedicated to the god of the moon.

Over the centuries, the mud structure began to erode and it was restored by King Nebuchadnezzar II, ruler of Babylonia, in the 6th century BC.

THE MAYAN PYRAMIDS OF TIKAL

From 300 through 900 AD, Tikal was an important center for the Maya people. They constructed massive monuments in this location, which is modern-day Peten, Guatemala. There are five temples constructed as pyramids and the tallest has a temple dedicated to the two-headed serpent, one of their gods.

THE PYRAMID OF TIKAL

This stepped pyramid temple has a height of 213 feet. After the Maya left the site, these beautiful structures were overtaken by the rainforest and were forgotten for over eight centuries. In the 1850s, explorers from Europe found them and archaeologists began to dig at the site.

THE PYRAMID OF CESTIUS

This pyramid was built in Rome, Italy to provide a tomb for Gaius Cestius Epulo, who was a type of government official called a magistrate. There is an inscription to him and his heirs on this steep narrow pyramid, which was built in 12 BC and took workers about a year to construct. It's made of concrete blocks that were covered over with white marble. Inside there are paintings adorning the walls.

SUMMARY

In ancient times, many cultures created pyramids as tombs for their rulers and temples to their gods. The pyramids sometimes had smooth sides or were built with stepped sides or layered terraces. Pyramids provided a stable structure for construction and they also rose above the landscape as manmade mountains. Many of these ancient structures still stand today and are a testament to the architectural design and construction skills of ancient civilizations.

Awesome! Now that you've read about pyramids around the world you may want to read about other architectural wonders in the Baby Professor book Amazing Wonders Around the Globe! | Wonders Of The World | Children's Reference Books.

82552625R00040